# Spiritual Warfare Pray Book:

# Powerful Prayers to Overcome Darkness

PUBLISHED BY Fr. Michael Miles

Golden Folio Editions – Fr. Michael Miles

© **Copyright 2025 - All rights reserved.**

All introductions, analyses, and commentaries contained within this book may not be reproduced, duplicated, or transmitted without direct written permission from the author or the publisher. Under no circumstances will any blame or legal responsibility be held against the publisher or author for any damages, reparation, or monetary loss due to the information contained within this book, either directly or indirectly.

**Legal Notice:**

This book is only for personal use. You cannot amend, distribute, sell, use, quote, or paraphrase any part of the introductions, analyses, or commentaries within this book, without the consent of the author or publisher.

**Disclaimer Notice:**

Please note the information contained within this document is for educational and entertainment purposes only. All efforts have been executed to present accurate, up-to-date, reliable, complete information. No warranties of any kind are declared or implied. Readers acknowledge that the author is not engaged in the rendering of legal, financial, medical, or professional advice. The content within this book has been derived from various sources. Please consult a licensed professional before attempting any techniques outlined in this book.

By reading this document, the reader agrees that under no circumstances is the author responsible for any losses, direct or indirect, that are incurred as a result of the use of the information contained within this document, including, but not limited to, errors, omissions, or inaccuracies.

# Spiritual Warfare

# Table of contents

Introduction .................................................................................... 5

Chapter I ........................................................................................ 12
    I.I Prayer to Wear the Full Armor of God ............................ 12
    I.II Prayer for Discernment in Battle ................................... 14
    I.III Morning Consecration to the Cross ............................ 16

Chapter II ..................................................................................... 18
    II.I Prayer of Authority Over the Enemy ............................ 18
    II.II Prayer to Break Curses and Generational Bonds ....... 20
    II.III Binding and Loosing Prayer ...................................... 22

Chapter III .................................................................................... 24
    III.I Prayer for Protection with the Precious Blood ........... 24
    III.II Prayer of Cleansing After Temptation or Sin ............. 27
    III.III Intercessory Prayer Using the Blood of Jesus .......... 29

Chapter IV ................................................................................... 31
    IV.I The Rosary of Liberation ............................................ 31
    IV.II The Consecration to the Immaculate Heart ............... 35
    IV.III Prayer of Refuge Under Mary's Mantle .................... 37

Chapter V .................................................................................... 39
    V.I The Chaplet of St. Michael .......................................... 39
    V.II Prayer for Angelic Reinforcements ............................. 42
    V.III The Litany of the Angels ............................................ 44

Chapter VI ................................................................................... 46
    VI.I Prayer of Contrition Before Confession ...................... 46
    VI.II Prayer of Thanksgiving After Confession .................. 48

## Golden Folio Editions – Fr. Michael Miles

 VI.III Prayer to Guard the Senses ............................................................. 50

## Chapter VII ............................................................................................. 53
 VII.I Prayer Before Receiving Communion ........................................... 53
 VII.II Prayer of Adoration Before the Tabernacle ................................ 55
 VII.III Prayer After Communion: Soldier's Benediction ..................... 57

## Chapter VIII ........................................................................................... 59
 VIII.I Prayer to Close Spiritual Portals .................................................. 59
 VIII.II The Litany of Light ....................................................................... 61
 VIII.III Prayer of Peace for the Household ............................................ 63

## Chapter IX ............................................................................................. 65
 IX.I Prayer for a Loved One in Crisis .................................................... 65
 IX.II Prayer for Those Under Spiritual Attack ..................................... 67
 IX.III Prayer for the Church Under Siege .............................................. 69

## Chapter X ............................................................................................... 71
 X.I Prayer of Praise for Breakthrough ................................................... 71
 X.II Declaration of Identity in Christ .................................................... 73
 X.III Litany of Victory ............................................................................. 75

## Conclusion ............................................................................................. 77

# Introduction

*Spiritual Warfare Pray Book: Powerful Prayers to Overcome Darkness*

The Christian life, in its fullest expression, is not merely a path of inner peace and moral instruction. It is also a battle—a spiritual conflict that has raged since the fall of man and continues to unfold in every age, every heart, every family, and every corner of the Church. This book is born from that battlefield. It is offered not as a manual of fear or superstition, but as a weapon of hope, discipline, and divine strength—rooted firmly in the Catholic tradition and forged in the furnace of centuries of lived faith.

This *Spiritual Warfare Pray Book* was written to equip Catholics with a powerful and reverent tool for daily combat in the spiritual realm. Many today are unaware of the subtle but persistent forces that seek to undermine their peace, derail their vocations, and corrupt their relationship with God. These forces—whether they come through temptation, despair, confusion, or hidden malice—often strike in silence and darkness. Yet Christ, the Light of the world, has not left His people defenseless. He has entrusted to His Church a treasury of prayer, sacrament, and communion—a heritage of holiness and power that spans two millennia. This book draws from that treasury, not to add anything new to the faith, but to help reclaim what is already ours through baptism, through Christ, and through the sacred liturgy.

At its heart, spiritual warfare is not a fight for domination or destruction, but a struggle for fidelity and freedom. It is the resistance of the soul to the seductions of sin, the lies of the evil one, and the despair that can so easily take root in the human heart. The Catechism of the Catholic Church teaches that the whole of man's history has been marked by the combat between good and evil, "a dramatic situation of 'the whole world [which] is in the power of the evil one'" (CCC 409). But this is not a fight to be feared. It is one in which victory is assured—if we stand under the banner of Christ, wielding the weapons He has placed in our hands.

This book is more than a collection of prayers. It is a daily companion for the faithful, meant to nourish both personal and communal devotion. Within these pages are time-tested invocations to the saints, Scriptural proclamations of truth, traditional deliverance prayers, and intercessions fortified by centuries of Catholic spiritual heritage. It also offers guidance on how and when to pray—not in a rigid or burdensome way, but as a rhythm of life that fosters intimacy with God, clarity of purpose, and peace of soul. Morning prayers to begin the day in grace and intention. Evening prayers to examine conscience, seek protection, and return to rest under the mantle of Our Lady. Special prayers "before battle"—whether that be a difficult meeting, a spiritual dry spell, a temptation, or even an attack sensed in the interior life. These rhythms anchor the soul, drawing it out of chaos and into communion with the Divine.

But what is spiritual warfare, really? And how does one know if one is experiencing it?

Spiritual warfare, in Catholic theology, refers to the conflict between the Kingdom of God and the forces of evil, both in the world and within the human soul. It is not a metaphorical flourish. It is a real and present conflict, evidenced throughout Scripture, witnessed in the lives of the saints, and acknowledged clearly by the Magisterium of the Church. This warfare is not waged with swords or political power, but through prayer, penance, sacramental life, and fidelity to Christ.

At the same time, it is important to distinguish spiritual warfare from purely psychological or emotional struggles. Not every moment of discouragement, depression, or anxiety stems from a demonic source. The human person is a complex union of body and soul, and we do not deny the need for mental health care, emotional healing, and proper self-knowledge. Psychological wounds may need therapy. Chemical imbalances may require medication. But even in those cases, prayer is not absent. Grace builds upon nature. A spiritually grounded person who is also emotionally well-integrated is better able to discern the true nature of their suffering and resist the lies of the enemy. In all things, discernment is key, and discernment flows from prayer, Scripture, Church teaching, and, when necessary, spiritual direction.

The enemy—whom the Church has always recognized as personal and real, not symbolic or abstract—is subtle. He does not always announce himself with dramatic manifestations. More often, he whispers in half-truths. He plants seeds of doubt, fear, resentment, and shame. He isolates. He confuses. And he accuses. But Christ, the Good Shepherd, does not abandon His sheep to the wolves. He has given us everything we need to overcome: the sacraments, especially Confession and the Eucharist; the intercession of the saints and angels; the power of sacred Scripture; and the authority of prayer spoken in faith.

These are not optional ornaments of Catholicism. They are armor. And it is time we learn again to wear them.

Central to this renewal is a return to structured, intentional prayer—not as a formula, but as formation. The saints did not become saints by accident. They lived by rhythm. They immersed themselves in the Psalms. They invoked the name of Jesus. They fasted. They spoke with authority, not because they were strong in themselves, but because they had yielded their lives entirely to Christ. This book is meant to help ordinary Catholics do the same, even in the context of busy, modern life. It is a companion for parents raising children in a chaotic culture; for students battling confusion in identity and purpose; for priests and religious confronting temptations and discouragement; for those suffering silently in marriages, workplaces, or parishes. The prayers contained here can be whispered in a moment of temptation, sung in communal worship, or proclaimed with holy boldness in the privacy of one's room. The important thing is that they are prayed—with faith, with intention, and with trust in God's power.

Using this book effectively begins with humility. One does not need to feel "worthy" or spiritually elite to begin. In fact, those who feel most weak and weary are often closest to God's heart. Begin simply. Choose a time in the morning—perhaps before breakfast or on the commute to work—to consecrate the day, invoke the angels, and ask for divine wisdom. In the evening, set aside a moment of silence to review the day, thank the Lord, ask pardon, and request protection during the night. In moments of acute spiritual conflict—whether temptation, fear, confusion, or habitual sin—turn to the "before battle" prayers, and do so with confidence, knowing that your voice is heard.

This book is also intended to be used in community. Husbands and wives can pray these prayers together, sealing their homes in spiritual authority. Parents can pray over their children, reclaiming their authority as the first educators and protectors of the domestic church. Prayer groups, religious communities, and parish apostolates can gather to invoke Heaven in one voice—reminding one another that they are not alone in the fight. There is power when the Body of Christ prays together, just as the early Church did in the upper room, waiting for the Spirit to fall. This is not mere symbolism. It is a living reality.

One of the great errors of our time is to see evil only in political or cultural terms. Certainly, ideologies, systems, and structures can be corrupted. But spiritual warfare goes deeper. It targets the soul. It aims to pull us away from prayer, make us question God's goodness, and ultimately despair of salvation. Yet Christ has already triumphed. The Cross is the definitive victory. Our task is to stand firm in that victory, not as passive observers, but as active participants in the redemption of the world.

The sacraments, above all, remain our most potent weapons. The sacrament of Reconciliation is the battlefield where Satan's accusations are silenced. The Eucharist is the banquet of victory—the Body and Blood of the One who has crushed the serpent's head. Baptism, Confirmation, Marriage, Holy Orders, Anointing of the Sick—each in its way confers grace and strength to resist evil and to live in the fullness of God's will. But prayer is what sustains us between the sacraments. It is our breath, our nourishment, our shield.

In praying the prayers of this book, remember that the words themselves are not magic formulas. Their power lies not in perfect recitation but in the faith of the one who prays them. Pray with authority, not because you feel powerful, but because Christ is powerful and has given you access to His name. Speak Scripture aloud. Call on the saints by name. Plead the Precious Blood. Invoke the Blessed Virgin Mary, whose humility and fiat crushed the ancient serpent more surely than any sword. Her presence in this book is not a poetic gesture—it is a strategic one. The Church has long understood Mary as the terror of demons, and countless testimonies affirm her role in deliverance and protection.

This book was not written to replace the liturgy, the Divine Office, or the daily Rosary. Rather, it complements them. It is a tool among many, a supplement for those who feel they are in a fight, who sense the darkness pressing in, and who long to pray but don't always know how. If it can help even one soul to rise in prayer instead of fall into despair, it will have fulfilled its purpose.

You are not alone. The Church on earth is surrounded by the Church in Heaven. The angels walk beside you. The saints intercede for you. Christ Himself prays for you at the right hand of the Father. All of Heaven watches and waits for each of us to rise again in faith, to take up the armor of God, and to fight—not in fear, but in love.

Let this book be a weapon in your hands, a light in your darkness, and a companion on your journey to holiness.

In Christ our Victor,
+
**Fr. Michael Miles**

# Spiritual Warfare

Golden Folio Editions – Fr. Michael Miles

# Chapter I

**Armor of God – The Foundation of Protection**
*"Put on the full armor of God, so that you can take your stand against the devil's schemes." –* Ephesians 6:11

## I.I Prayer to Wear the Full Armor of God

Heavenly Father,
In the name of Jesus Christ, I rise this day and place myself beneath Your mighty protection. Clothe me, O Lord, with the full armor You have given through grace, that I may stand firm against every assault of the enemy and walk in the freedom of Your truth.

Gird my waist with the **belt of truth**.
Let honesty rule my thoughts, words, and actions. Guard me from deception, from lies whispered by the evil one, and from the temptation to compromise.

Place upon me the **breastplate of righteousness**.
Not my own merit, but the righteousness of Christ. May my heart be protected from bitterness, pride, impurity, and despair. Create in me a clean heart, O God, and renew a steadfast spirit within me.

Let my feet be shod with the **gospel of peace**.
Guide every step I take today. Make me a bearer of Your peace in a world of unrest. Grant me courage to proclaim Your truth and compassion to walk humbly with others.

## Spiritual Warfare

Raise over me the **shield of faith**.
Let no flaming arrow of doubt, fear, accusation, or discouragement pierce through. Strengthen my faith in Your promises, O Lord, and help me to trust in Your power when I am weak.

Place upon my head the **helmet of salvation**.
Guard my mind from confusion, pride, anxiety, and the voices that contradict Your word. Let the hope of eternal life be my constant vision and the joy of my salvation my strength.

Place in my hands the **sword of the Spirit**, which is the Word of God.
Let Scripture be always on my lips, in my mind, and in my heart. Teach me to wield it with wisdom, to silence the enemy, and to proclaim Your truth with boldness and love.

Holy Spirit, be my guide and strength today.
Help me to walk not in the flesh, but by Your power. Deliver me from temptation, sustain me in trial, and consecrate my thoughts, words, and deeds to Your glory.

Lord Jesus, I surrender this day to You.
Let every moment, every challenge, and every encounter be an offering of love to You. Send forth Your angels to surround me, and let Your presence go before me.

I put on the full armor of God. I take my stand against every plan of darkness.
In the name of the Father, and of the Son, and of the Holy Spirit. Amen.

## I.II Prayer for Discernment in Battle

Lord of Light,
You are the Shepherd who calls His sheep by name, and Your voice is truth. In this day of battle, grant me the grace to hear You clearly, to know what comes from You, and to reject what is not. Sharpen the eyes of my soul, that I may see beyond appearances and recognize the snares that lie hidden in shadows.

When confusion clouds my path, be my clarity.
When the enemy twists Your words and sows doubt in my heart, remind me of Your unchanging promises. Let no false light lead me astray, no flattering voice draw me from the narrow way. Where the world speaks comfort at the cost of holiness, give me the courage to walk in the truth that wounds in order to heal.

Guard me from spiritual deception—from every spirit that does not confess You, Jesus, come in the flesh and risen in glory. Teach me to test all things by Your word, to remain rooted in the teachings of the Church, and to seek the counsel of the wise.

When fear tempts me to compromise, let Your truth make me bold.
When pride blinds my judgment, humble me gently.
When I am weary and tempted to choose what is easy over what is right, strengthen me with heavenly wisdom.

Let no spiritual trap take hold of me today.
Preserve me, O Lord, from every scheme dressed in good intentions, from every voice that flatters but does not edify,

## Spiritual Warfare

from every movement that excites but does not sanctify. Teach me to recognize the fruit of the Spirit, and to walk always in the light of Your face.

You are my Rock, my Fortress, and my Guide.
Lead me in Your truth, and guard my steps in every hour of this day. In Your name, Jesus, I pray. Amen.

## I.III Morning Consecration to the Cross

O Jesus, Crucified Lord,
At the break of this new day, I come before Your holy Cross, the throne of mercy, the sign of victory, and the source of my salvation. I bow my life before You.

I offer You my mind.
Let no thought rise in me today that does not honor You. Purify my intellect; sanctify my imagination; fill my memory with Your truth. Let all distraction be cast out in Your name. Seal my mind with Your holy wounds.

I offer You my heart.
Cleanse it of pride, envy, resentment, and desire for control. Fill it with Your meekness and love. Teach me to feel what You feel, to love what You love, and to be moved by what moves Your Sacred Heart. Make my affections pure, ordered, and directed to Your will alone.

I offer You my body.
Strengthen my hands for Your service, my feet to walk in Your path, my mouth to speak only blessing, and my eyes to see with compassion. Let my body be a temple of the Holy Spirit, free from impurity, laziness, or excess. May all I do today glorify You in soul and flesh.

By Your holy Passion, protect me.
By Your Precious Blood, cover me.
By the power of Your Cross, bind me to Yourself.

## Spiritual Warfare

Guard me from all evil—visible and invisible. Shield me from harm and temptation. Let no part of me serve the enemy in thought, word, or deed. Today, I choose You. I bind my heart to Your Sacred Heart. I bind my life to Your holy will. May this day unfold according to Your purpose, not mine.

I consecrate this day, every hour, every task, every encounter, to You and to the glory of the Father. I entrust myself to Mary, Your Mother and mine, to guide me and shield me beneath her mantle.

In the name of the Father, and of the Son, and of the Holy Spirit. Amen.

# Chapter II

**Deliverance from Evil Spirits**
*"Our struggle is not against flesh and blood..."* – Ephesians 6:12

## II.I Prayer of Authority Over the Enemy

In the name of Jesus Christ, my Lord and Savior,
I stand today in the power of His cross, in the triumph of His resurrection, and in the glory of His ascension. I proclaim that Jesus is Lord of my life—of my mind, my body, my soul, and all that I am. Through His Precious Blood, shed for me, I have been redeemed, cleansed, and made new.

By the authority given to me in baptism and in the name of Jesus Christ,
I now speak against every spirit that is not from God. I renounce all darkness, every lie, every whisper of the enemy. I reject all fear, confusion, hatred, lust, pride, despair, and division. I sever every tie—known or unknown—to the enemy's influence. In the name of Jesus, I break all permission I have ever given, whether by sin, word, deed, or consent.

Jesus, I ask You to cover me now with Your Precious Blood. Let it flow over my mind, my heart, my body, my home, my family, and all that You have entrusted to me. Cleanse me from all oppression. Break every chain. Scatter the enemy. Let no evil spirit have power or claim over me, for I belong to You alone.

# Spiritual Warfare

Saint Michael the Archangel, defend me in battle.
Be my protection against the wickedness and snares of the devil. Cast into hell every evil spirit who prowls through the world seeking the ruin of souls. Mighty Prince of the Heavenly Host, come with your legions of angels and drive far from me every force of darkness.

Holy Spirit, fill every place now emptied.
Where fear was, pour peace. Where confusion lingered, give clarity. Where darkness crept in, shine Your light. Seal every door, every thought, every part of me with Your presence.

I place my trust in the power of Christ.
No weapon formed against me shall prosper, for I am a child of God, purchased by the Blood of the Lamb. Let every unclean spirit now depart in the name and power of Jesus Christ, never to return.

I am Yours, Lord Jesus. I give You all authority over my life. Let Your kingdom reign in me. Let Your name be glorified. Let Your will be done, now and forever. Amen.

## II.II Prayer to Break Curses and Generational Bonds

Eternal Father,
In the name of Jesus Christ, Your Son, and by the power of the Holy Spirit, I come before You today as Your child, redeemed by the waters of baptism and sealed with the anointing of confirmation. I thank You for the grace of being born again in Christ, made a new creation through His sacrifice and Your mercy.

Standing in that identity, I now bring before You my family line—my ancestry, both maternal and paternal. I ask You to stretch forth Your hand and uncover every hidden chain, every inherited bond, every curse spoken or unspoken that has taken root in my bloodline. If there are sins, vows, oaths, superstitions, or occult practices that have opened doors across generations, I renounce them now in the name of Jesus.

In the authority of my baptism, I reject and cast off every stronghold that has passed through my family: every spirit of addiction, anger, hatred, division, fear, infirmity, bitterness, rebellion, idolatry, or impurity. I break their power in the name of Jesus. I declare that they no longer have a claim or voice in my life or the lives of my descendants.

Lord, let the light of Christ now shine through every generation. Wash my family line clean in the Precious Blood of Jesus—from the first to the last. Heal every wound passed down. Cleanse every dark root. Uproot every lie planted by the enemy, and replace it with Your truth. Let no curse continue. Let no darkness remain. Let the blessings of faith, hope, and love flow freely from one generation to the next.

I claim the promises of baptism. I stand in the grace of the sacraments.
And I ask You, Lord, to pour out Your Spirit upon my family: on the living and the departed, and upon those yet to come. Let Christ be enthroned in our lineage. Let Your mercy redeem our past, sanctify our present, and bless our future.

In Jesus' name I pray. Amen.

## II.III Binding and Loosing Prayer

Lord Jesus Christ,
With faith in Your authority and trust in Your Word, I come before You now to take spiritual authority over all that is not of You. In Your holy name, I bind every spirit of fear that seeks to paralyze, confuse, or dominate my thoughts. I bind the spirit of confusion that clouds judgment and distorts truth. I bind the spirit of pride that hardens the heart and resists correction. I bind all spirits that rebel against Your will or speak lies into my soul.

In Your name, Jesus, I render them powerless, mute, and without ground.
By the power of Your Cross and the Blood You shed, I command them to depart, to leave this place, and to return to the foot of the Cross for judgment. I revoke their access, I renounce their lies, and I place my full trust in Your victory.

In the same authority, I now loose what is of You.
I loose the peace that surpasses all understanding to reign in my mind and home. I loose joy—deep and unwavering—to flood my heart where sorrow once ruled. I loose the gift of faith to grow strong within me, rooted in Your Word and unshaken by storms. I loose the power of divine love to flow through every wound, every memory, and every part of my life that needs healing.

Lord, seal this prayer in the power of Your Cross.
Cover me and all who belong to me with Your Precious Blood. Let no retaliation come, no backlash, no return of what has been

## Spiritual Warfare

cast away. Surround me with Your angels, and let the light of Your presence remain.

You are my deliverer, my fortress, and my strength.
I rest in Your promise and walk forward in Your freedom.
In the name of the Father, and of the Son, and of the Holy Spirit. Amen.

# Chapter III

**The Power of the Precious Blood**
*"They triumphed over him by the blood of the Lamb..."* –
Revelation 12:11

## III.I Prayer for Protection with the Precious Blood

Lord Jesus Christ,
Son of the Living God, I kneel before You today, calling upon the power of Your Precious Blood. You, the spotless Lamb, poured out Your Blood for my salvation, for the healing of the nations, and for the destruction of the works of the devil. It is not by my strength that I stand, but by the Blood You shed upon the Cross—pure, holy, and victorious.

I plead Your Precious Blood now over my life.
Cover my body, my soul, and my spirit. Wash me in Your mercy. Let every part of me be sealed in Your Blood: my mind, that no lie may take root; my heart, that no hatred may enter; my eyes, that they may remain fixed on You; my mouth, that it may speak only truth and blessing; my hands, that they may serve with humility; and my feet, that they may walk only in Your ways.

I plead Your Blood over my home.
Over every room, every doorway, every window. Let Your Blood be upon the walls and thresholds. Let it shield all who dwell here from every spirit of division, fear, violence, unrest,

## Spiritual Warfare

or temptation. Let Your Blood silence every unclean voice and drive out all darkness. Sanctify this place with the echo of Calvary and the triumph of Your resurrection.

I plead Your Blood over my loved ones—
my family, my friends, all those I carry in my heart. Surround them with a hedge of protection. Let the enemy find no entry, no permission, no ground. May Your Blood speak louder than every curse, louder than every lie, louder than the accuser's voice. Let Your mercy fall upon each soul like dew from Heaven, refreshing, healing, and restoring what is broken.

Lord, I see in faith the shield of Your Blood—
a covering that no darkness can cross, a mantle that no evil can penetrate. Let it be as a wall of fire around me and a light within me. Let it speak in the spiritual realm: "This one belongs to Christ." I accept no compromise with evil. I declare Your dominion over my life. I yield all to You—my possessions, my relationships, my past, present, and future. All is under the Blood.

Precious Blood of Jesus, protect me.
Precious Blood of Jesus, cleanse me.
Precious Blood of Jesus, claim me for the Kingdom.

Today, I walk under the covering of Your sacrifice.
I live not in fear, but in the confidence of Your victory.
I proclaim that You are Lord—of every hour, every breath, and every battle.

In Your Most Holy Name I pray. Amen.

Golden Folio Editions – Fr. Michael Miles

## III.II Prayer of Cleansing After Temptation or Sin

Lord Jesus Christ,
I come before You with a heart that knows its need. I confess my weakness, my failure, and my sin. I have fallen short, not only in action, but in thought, desire, and intention. I have turned from what is holy and allowed the enemy to whisper lies into my heart. Yet I do not run from You—I run to You, because You are mercy itself.

By the Blood You poured out on the Cross,
wash me clean. Let not my sin define me, but let Your mercy renew me. I do not trust in my efforts, but in Your infinite compassion. Where shame tries to cling, clothe me with Your righteousness. Where the wound of temptation has cut deep, pour the balm of Your Precious Blood until I am healed.

Jesus, make me whole again.
Restore the innocence that sin tried to steal. Quiet the voices that accuse, and replace them with the voice of the Good Shepherd. Remove the residue of the battle. Purify my mind, calm my emotions, and reclaim every place that darkness tried to touch.

You are the Lamb of God who takes away the sins of the world. Take mine. I give it to You now, freely, in sorrow and in trust. And I receive again the grace of Your forgiveness, purchased at such a cost. May I rise from this moment with a heart made clean, a conscience at peace, and a spirit renewed for the path ahead.

Cover me in Your Blood, Lord. Hide me in Your wounds.
Let nothing unclean remain. Let no power of hell accuse me.
Let Your mercy be my armor, and Your love my strength.

In the name of the Father, and of the Son, and of the Holy Spirit. Amen.

## III.III Intercessory Prayer Using the Blood of Jesus

Lord Jesus,
You who laid down Your life for the salvation of the world, I come before You now on behalf of those I carry in my heart. You see each one—their battles, their wounds, their sins, their blindness. I offer no judgment, only prayer. And I offer it through the only means strong enough to save: Your Most Precious Blood.

I plead Your Blood over the souls of the lost.
Over those who walk in darkness, knowingly or not. Over those hardened by pride, wounded by betrayal, numbed by the world. I ask You to break the chains that bind them. Tear down the walls that keep them far from You. Let Your Blood speak louder than their rebellion, louder than their guilt, louder than their despair.

I invoke the power of Your sacrifice over their lives.
Protect them from every evil influence. Surround them with Your light. Send holy angels to guard them, and place on their path voices that call them home. Where the enemy has claimed ground, let Your Blood reclaim it. Where lies have been sown, let Your truth rise like dawn.

Soften their hearts, Lord.
Let the hardness melt in the warmth of Your mercy. Let memories of grace return. Let hope awaken again. Stir in them a longing they cannot explain—a hunger for the truth, a thirst for Your love.

Jesus, You are the High Priest who intercedes for us at the right hand of the Father.
Unite my prayer to Yours now. I ask not by my merit, but by Your wounds. Let Your Blood flow into the lives of those who most need it. Rescue, restore, redeem.

For Your glory, Lord—not mine. For their freedom, not my comfort. For the joy of Heaven, not the praise of men. I trust in Your mercy. I entrust them to Your heart.

In the name of the Father, and of the Son, and of the Holy Spirit. Amen.

# Chapter IV

**Marian Protection in Battle**
*"In dangers, in doubts, in difficulties, think of Mary, call upon Mary..."* – St. Bernard of Clairvaux

## IV.I The Rosary of Liberation

O Blessed Virgin Mary,
Mother of God and Queen of Angels, I take refuge under your mantle today, not as a stranger, but as your child, entrusted to your care by the words of your Son from the Cross. In the trials of life, in the hidden battles of the soul, and in the fierce combat against the powers of darkness, I call upon your name with confidence. As I pray this Rosary, I unite each mystery to a cry for deliverance—for myself, for my family, and for all those weighed down by spiritual oppression.

In the name of Jesus Christ and through your maternal intercession, I pray this Rosary not as a repetition of words, but as a weapon against all that enslaves the human heart. May each Hail Mary be a blow against the enemy. May each mystery proclaim the triumph of grace. May your heel, O Immaculate One, continue to crush the head of the ancient serpent.

**The Joyful Mysteries** are offered for liberation from the roots of sin.
Through the Annunciation, I pray for the grace to welcome God's will over every temptation to self-rule. Through the Visitation, I pray that joy may replace despair in every soul

gripped by darkness. Through the Nativity, I ask that Christ be born anew in the hearts of those far from God. Through the Presentation, I offer all hidden bondages to the light of God's law. Through the Finding in the Temple, I pray for the return of every lost soul to the heart of the Church.

**The Sorrowful Mysteries** are offered for those enslaved by fear, shame, or torment.
In the Agony in the Garden, I place before God every struggle with despair and spiritual paralysis. In the Scourging at the Pillar, I plead for healing from wounds caused by sin and from affliction in body or soul. In the Crowning with Thorns, I ask for the renewal of minds held captive by lies. In the Carrying of the Cross, I pray for strength for those overwhelmed by addiction, guilt, or trauma. In the Crucifixion, I unite all suffering to Christ's redeeming Passion and claim freedom through His Blood.

**The Glorious Mysteries** are offered for the victory of God's reign over every stronghold.
In the Resurrection, I proclaim that no chain is stronger than the risen Christ. In the Ascension, I entrust all situations to the authority of Jesus enthroned in glory. In the Descent of the Holy Spirit, I call for fire to fall on those in spiritual bondage. In the Assumption of Mary, I ask that all who suffer may be lifted into grace through your intercession. In the Coronation of Mary, I proclaim you, O Queen of Heaven and Earth, as the terror of demons and the refuge of the faithful.

O Mary, my Mother,
Wrap your mantle around me.
Defend me from every assault of the enemy.

## Spiritual Warfare

Guide my hand as I pray.
May this Rosary echo through the heavens,
May it resound in the courts of angels,
And may it bring light to every shadowed place in my soul.

I pray not alone, but with you,
I fight not in fear, but in faith,
And I trust that through your powerful intercession,
Chains will be broken, lives will be restored,
And the name of Jesus will be glorified.

Amen.

Golden Folio Editions – Fr. Michael Miles

# IV.II The Consecration to the Immaculate Heart

O Immaculate Heart of Mary,
Mother most pure, I come before you today with full confidence in your motherly love and the power of your intercession. I consecrate myself entirely to you—my body, my soul, my thoughts, my desires, my joys, my sufferings, my past, my future, and every moment of this day. Nothing do I withhold from you, O Mother, for I know that whatever is placed in your hands is made holy and returned to God.

I entrust to you all my spiritual battles.
Every struggle hidden in the silence of my heart, every temptation that presses at the door, every wound that still cries out for healing—I place it under your care. Be my Advocate in Heaven, my defense on earth, and my companion on the path of holiness. Teach me to fight not with anger but with trust, not with fear but with surrender, not with despair but with perseverance in grace.

O Virgin most powerful, crush the head of the serpent under your heel.
You, who were never touched by sin, whose heart is spotless before God, wield a power no demon can resist. Drive far from me all shadows of evil. Let no unclean spirit linger near. Let every curse be broken and every tie to darkness undone through your immaculate presence.

Help me to live this consecration not as a one-time prayer, but as a total offering renewed each day. Let your heart beat in mine. Let your virtues live in me. Let your gaze turn my eyes to

Christ in all things. Keep me always close, never distant. Let me rest in your heart, and through you, enter more deeply into the Sacred Heart of Jesus, your Son and my Lord.

O Mary, my Mother and Queen, I am all yours.
Now and forever, I give myself to your Immaculate Heart.
Protect me. Guide me. Triumph in me for the glory of God.

Amen.

## IV.III Prayer of Refuge Under Mary's Mantle

O Mary, gentle Mother,
When the storm surrounds me and the arrows of the enemy fly, I seek no other shelter but you. Stretch forth your mantle, O Virgin of mercy, and draw me beneath it. Let me rest in the folds of your protection, hidden from the pursuit of the evil one, sheltered from the chaos of the world, guarded from all that seeks to disturb my peace.

In this place of refuge, I breathe again.
Though the battle may rage around me, I am not afraid, for your presence calms every fear. Cover my mind, that no torment may take hold. Cover my heart, that no bitterness may grow. Cover my body, that no harm may come. Let your mantle be light to my eyes, strength to my spirit, and consolation to my soul.

Mother most tender, speak for me when I cannot find the words. Intercede for me with the power entrusted to you by your Son. Where I am weak, ask for strength. Where I am lost, beg for guidance. Where I am afflicted, obtain healing. Where I am tempted, draw near with your maternal grace and shield me from every fall.

O Mary, Star of the Sea,
Guide me through these troubled waters.
O Tower of Ivory,
Lift me above the shadows.
O Refuge of Sinners,
Receive me into your arms and never let me go.

Wrap me now, Blessed Mother, in your mantle of peace. Let it remain upon me throughout this day, through every hour, every trial, and every joy. Lead me safely to the Heart of your Son, where all battles end in victory and all wounds find rest.

Amen.

# Chapter V

**Saint Michael and the Heavenly Hosts**
*"Defend us in battle, be our safeguard against the wickedness..."* – Prayer to St. Michael

# V.I The Chaplet of St. Michael

O Prince of the Heavenly Host,
Saint Michael, great defender of the people of God, I turn to you with reverence and urgency. In a world surrounded by unseen conflict and spiritual snares, I call upon your mighty intercession. Through you, the battle cry of Heaven still resounds—*Who is like God?*—and in your name, I entrust this chaplet as a cry for protection, for purity, for perseverance in the fight against evil.

This Chaplet is prayed not out of fear, but with confidence in the power of God who commands the hosts of Heaven. As I offer each salutation, I call upon the nine choirs of angels whom God created in glory, to assist, defend, and guide those who walk the narrow path of salvation.

I begin in the name of the Father, and of the Son, and of the Holy Spirit. Amen.

**On the introductory medal**, I offer this invocation:
O glorious Saint Michael, Chief and Commander of the Heavenly Hosts, be my protector in the combat of this life. Defend me from temptation, preserve me in purity, and

strengthen me in every spiritual battle. Accompany me now as I call upon the choirs of angels with love and devotion.

**For each of the nine choirs**, I pray one Our Father and three Hail Marys, with these intentions:

In honor of the **Seraphim**, I ask for the fire of divine love to burn away every attachment to sin and ignite my soul with zeal for God.

In honor of the **Cherubim**, I seek clarity and purity of mind, that all deception and confusion be cast out in the light of divine truth.

In honor of the **Thrones**, I pray for humility and peace, and that I may remain surrendered to God's perfect will even in trial.

In honor of the **Dominions**, I ask for strength to govern my passions and to resist the temptation to control what belongs to God alone.

In honor of the **Virtues**, I pray for courage in suffering, constancy in prayer, and victory over every affliction.

In honor of the **Powers**, I ask for deliverance from all oppression and for the breaking of chains both seen and unseen.

In honor of the **Principalities**, I pray for divine protection over nations, communities, families, and the Church, that order and truth may prevail.

# Spiritual Warfare

In honor of the **Archangels**, especially you, Saint Michael, I entrust all moments of temptation, doubt, and spiritual fatigue. Stand beside me when I am weak.

In honor of the **Angels**, my guardians and companions, I thank God for their unseen presence. May they guard my steps, whisper truth in silence, and guide me home.

**At the conclusion**, I pray:

O glorious Saint Michael, through this chaplet I place myself beneath your shield. Fight for me in every hidden battle. Cast from my life all that resists grace. Surround me with your angelic warriors. Let no evil enter, let no fear remain, and let no sin take root.

Guard my body, mind, and soul.
Be present in moments of decision, temptation, and suffering.
Lead me safely through the valley of darkness and into the light of the Kingdom.

I entrust all to God through you.
May this prayer rise as incense before the throne of Heaven.
And may my soul, defended by the hosts of angels, walk faithfully until the end.

Amen.

# V.II Prayer for Angelic Reinforcements

Heavenly Father,
Lord of Hosts and Creator of all that is seen and unseen, I call upon the aid You have ordained from the beginning: the holy angels who serve You with perfect obedience. In the name of Jesus Christ, I ask You to send forth Your legions—angels of light, purity, and fire—to surround me now.

Let these heavenly warriors stand guard at the corners of my life.
Dispatch them to encamp around my home, my family, my workplace, and every path I tread. Assign them, Lord, according to Your will. Let no threat—visible or invisible—cross the threshold You have sealed. Let no shadow rest upon what has been consecrated to You.

I call upon my guardian angel, given to me at birth.
Holy companion, faithful and silent guide, I ask you now to be vigilant. Strengthen me when I falter. Whisper truth when I am tempted. Shield me from every unseen danger. If I have ever grieved you by neglect or sin, I ask your pardon. I welcome your presence again with reverence and gratitude.

And I ask You, Lord, to send angels to those I love.
Place a guardian at the bedside of each family member. Let no fear disturb their rest, no evil pass near their spirit. Surround my home with a wall of angels. Let them ascend and descend as they did for Jacob, bearing messages, standing watch, waging war in silence. Let no curse endure. Let no lie remain. Let no enemy draw near.

# Spiritual Warfare

By Your authority, O God, I plead for angelic reinforcements. Not for vanity or spectacle, but for protection, for purity, and for the triumph of Your kingdom in my life. Let the angels who never sleep carry the shield I cannot lift, and let them praise You with me even in the midst of battle.

Amen.

## V.III The Litany of the Angels

Lord, have mercy.
Christ, have mercy.
Lord, have mercy.

God the Father of Heaven, have mercy on us.
God the Son, Redeemer of the world, have mercy on us.
God the Holy Spirit, have mercy on us.
Holy Trinity, one God, have mercy on us.

Holy Mary, Queen of Angels, pray for us.
Saint Michael the Archangel, leader of the heavenly host, pray for us.
Saint Gabriel the Archangel, bearer of glad tidings, pray for us.
Saint Raphael the Archangel, healer and guide, pray for us.
All holy Archangels, pray for us.
All holy Guardian Angels, pray for us.
You who stand before the throne of God, pray for us.
You who minister at the altar of Heaven, pray for us.
You who carry the prayers of the faithful to the Most High, pray for us.
You who war against the prince of darkness, pray for us.
You who never sleep, who watch with flaming swords, pray for us.
You who rejoice over one repentant sinner, pray for us.
You who strengthened Christ in the garden, pray for us.
You who comforted the saints in their hour of death, pray for us.

Angels of obedience, clothed in light, pray for us.
Angels of purity, who gaze upon God's face, pray for us.
Angels of strength, guardians of the weak, pray for us.

## Spiritual Warfare

Angels of silence, who stand in holy awe, pray for us.
Angels of glory, who sing without ceasing, pray for us.
Angels of warfare, defenders of the just, pray for us.

By the power of Your holy angels, O Lord,
Shield us in battle.
Lift us when we fall.
Whisper truth when lies surround us.
Strengthen us in the hour of trial.
Defend us from the enemy's snares.
Guide us on the path of holiness.

Lamb of God, who takes away the sins of the world, spare us, O Lord.
Lamb of God, who takes away the sins of the world, graciously hear us, O Lord.
Lamb of God, who takes away the sins of the world, have mercy on us.

God of angel armies, send Your angels to guard us in all our ways,
that we may dwell in peace and rise in victory.

Amen.

# Chapter VI

**Confession and Purity as Defense**
*"Confession is the soul's bath. Even a clean soul needs it..."* – St. Pio of Pietrelcina

## VI.I Prayer of Contrition Before Confession

Holy Spirit,
You who search the depths of the heart, come now and shine Your light upon my soul. Stir within me the truth I have buried, the moments I have resisted grace, the sins I have justified or ignored. Awaken in me a holy sorrow—not fear, not shame, but the sorrow of love wounded and longing to return.

Convict me, not to condemn, but to heal.
Reveal to me what I must confess. Let no sin remain hidden. Let no corner of my soul remain untouched by Your mercy. Show me not only my actions, but the roots beneath them. Teach me to see with honesty, to name my sins without excuse, and to come as a child to the Father's embrace.

Lord Jesus,
I am truly sorry for having offended You. Not only because I fear punishment, but because I have grieved the One who loves me beyond measure. You gave everything for me, and still I turned away. You opened Your heart, and I closed mine. But now I come back, not clinging to worthiness, but clinging to Your cross.

## Spiritual Warfare

Prepare me to confess with clarity and with courage.
Prepare me to receive absolution with humility and joy. Let my heart be fully open, fully surrendered, fully Yours. Cleanse me from within. Strip away all self-deception. Burn away what cannot remain, and pour into me what only You can give.

O Jesus, I trust in Your mercy.
Make me new. Let this confession not be routine, but a return. Let it be the moment grace flows freely, and my soul rises again in light. I am Yours, Lord. I was always Yours.

Amen.

## VI.II Prayer of Thanksgiving After Confession

Lord Jesus Christ,
I kneel before You in gratitude and awe. You have spoken the words of mercy, and my soul is made clean. What I could not undo, You have erased. What burdened my heart, You have lifted. What held me in shadow, You have brought into the light. Through the voice of Your priest, I have heard Your own voice: absolving, healing, restoring.

Thank You, Lord, for the gift of this sacrament,
where grace meets weakness, where love silences guilt, and where peace replaces torment. I rejoice not in my strength, but in Your mercy. I walk away from the confessional not as I entered—but lighter, freer, and filled with hope. Your Precious Blood has washed me. Your Spirit has renewed me. I belong to You once more.

Grant me now the grace to remain firm. Strengthen my will in temptation. Let no sin reclaim what You have cleansed. Let no lie undo what You have forgiven. Let no past voice drown out the freedom You have spoken over me. Build in me new habits of virtue. Teach me to walk in humility, vigilance, and love.

I offer reparation, Lord, for all harm I've caused—
to others, to myself, and to Your Sacred Heart. Teach me how to repair what was wounded. Let my sorrow bear fruit in action. I unite this offering with Yours, Jesus, that even my failings might become places of grace, and that Your mercy may be known through my witness.

Spiritual Warfare

Thank You, Lord, for never turning away.
Thank You for welcoming me again, not as a slave, but as a child. Keep me close. Keep me faithful. Keep me Yours.

Amen.

## VI.III Prayer to Guard the Senses

Heavenly Father,
You created me in Your image and breathed into me the breath of life. I offer back to You now my senses—every window of my soul—asking for Your protection, Your purity, and Your peace.

Guard my eyes, Lord,
that they may not wander toward vanity or impurity. Let them seek what is good, true, and worthy of praise. As it is written, "I will set no wicked thing before mine eyes" (Psalm 101:3). Let light, not darkness, enter through my gaze.

Guard my ears,
that I may not listen to slander, impurity, or deceit. Let me be deaf to the enemy's whisper and attentive to Your voice. "Incline your ear and come to Me," You say in Isaiah 55:3—let my ears be turned always to You.

Guard my mouth,
that I may speak no evil, entertain no gossip, and bless, not curse. Let my words build, heal, and proclaim truth. "Let no corrupt word proceed out of your mouth, but only such as is good for building up," as You teach in Ephesians 4:29. Purify my speech and tame my tongue.

Guard my touch,
that I may use my hands for works of mercy, not selfishness. Let every physical action reflect reverence and restraint. Let no act be careless or indulgent. May I carry my body as a temple of the Holy Spirit.

## Spiritual Warfare

Guard my thoughts,
that no bitterness, impurity, pride, or fear may take root. "Take every thought captive to obey Christ" (2 Corinthians 10:5), O Lord, and cleanse the sanctuary of my mind.

Grant me the virtues of chastity, sobriety, and self-control. Let me walk not by the desires of the flesh, but by the Spirit. Teach me to master my impulses, to fast from what pollutes, and to hunger for righteousness. Let Your Word be ever my sword and shield in temptation. May I say with the psalmist, "How can a young man keep his way pure? By guarding it according to Your word" (Psalm 119:9).

Wrap me in Your armor, Lord.
Let my senses be ordered, not ruled. Let my soul be watchful, not careless. Let my body glorify You in every glance, every word, every gesture.

Through the Immaculate Heart of Mary and in the name of Jesus Christ, I entrust myself wholly to Your protection.

Amen.

Golden Folio Editions – Fr. Michael Miles

# Chapter VII

**Eucharistic Warfare**
*"It is the Lord!"* – John 21:7

# VII.I Prayer Before Receiving Communion

Lord Jesus Christ,
I come to Your altar not as one worthy, but as one deeply in need. I approach the mystery of Your Body and Blood with trembling reverence and with the hope that what I lack, You will supply. My soul is a battleground, marked by struggles, failures, and fragile victories—but I invite You now to enter, not as a guest, but as King and Conqueror.

Prepare my heart to receive You.
Cleanse the dust from its corners, silence the noise within, and drive out anything that resists Your presence. Let no unconfessed sin linger in the shadows, no hidden pride hide behind the veil. Let my soul be stripped of false security and made open in humility, so that You may reign completely.

Lord, fill what is empty. Heal what is wounded.
I bring You every fear, every scar, every chain. I place before You the deep places in me that ache for truth and for wholeness. In this Holy Communion, I do not seek comfort only—I seek transformation. Let this sacrament be my healing, my strength, and my armor in the daily war against temptation and despair.

As I prepare to receive You, I enter into a covenant.
This is no mere moment. This is surrender. I bind myself to
You, Lord—not just in word, but in will, in desire, in obedience.
I give You permission to dwell in me fully. Let my heart be
Your tabernacle. Let my life bear witness that You live and
reign within me.

You who once said, "This is My Body," speak those words
again into my soul.
Speak life into what has withered. Speak peace where there has
been unrest. Speak courage where fear still lingers. Let this
Communion be a sword in my hand and a shield upon my heart.

I believe, Lord. I adore You. I trust You. I welcome You.
Come now into this unworthy servant, and let nothing ever
separate me from You again.

Amen.

## VII.II Prayer of Adoration Before the Tabernacle

Lord Jesus,
Here I am, kneeling in silence before You, hidden yet wholly present in the tabernacle. I do not need to see You with my eyes to know that You are here. I believe, Lord. I believe You wait for me, look upon me, and draw me closer even in this stillness.

I come to sit in Your Presence, not with many words, but with a heart open to adore. The world runs fast, voices press in from every side, and the weight of battle often leaves me weary. But here, in Your Presence, I find rest without escape, peace without illusion, strength without noise. You are the still point in the storm, the anchor of my soul, the light that no darkness can extinguish.

Reignite my courage in this sacred place.
Let this moment of adoration be a forge where fear is melted, faith is tempered, and love is renewed. Breathe into me again the strength I need to return to the field of life—clothed in grace, unshaken by temptation, and ready to stand for You.

Lord, I also bring before You those who do not believe, who do not know You hidden in this Holy Sacrament. For those who pass by the tabernacle unaware, for those who mock what they do not understand, for those whose hearts have grown cold—I beg You to open their eyes. Pour Your mercy upon them, that one day they too may kneel here in awe and love.

Let this hour in Your Presence bear fruit.
Let it become the quiet fire that lights the next battle. Let it

change me, Lord—not with noise, not with visions, but with the power of Your quiet love.

I adore You, Jesus. I trust You. I give You this moment, and every moment to come.

Amen.

## VII.III Prayer After Communion: Soldier's Benediction

Lord Jesus Christ,
You have come to me, and I am no longer my own. The King of Heaven has entered the frailty of my heart, and nothing will ever be the same. You have fed me with Your Body, filled me with Your Presence, and sealed me again in the covenant of Your love.

I thank You, my Eucharistic Lord, for this moment of sacred communion—
not as a feeling, but as a fact written in eternity. You have not only visited me; You have made Your dwelling in me. In this mystery, I am healed. In this gift, I am armed. In this union, I am made strong.

Now send me, Lord, back into the field.
Let me walk as one who carries You within—silent where silence is holy, bold where truth must be spoken, patient where hearts are hard, and fierce where justice is denied. Let me not fear the enemy, for I walk in the company of the Lamb. Let me not shrink from suffering, for I carry the sign of Your Cross.

You are my shield. You are my sword.
You are the banner I raise in the face of darkness. Let no power of hell steal this hour from me. Let no shadow cloud what You have planted. Let no trial make me forget that I have tasted victory in Your Flesh and Blood.

Seal my soul, Lord Jesus, with the mark of Your indwelling. May every step I take be a step in You. May every breath I draw be filled with grace. And may the echo of this Communion resound in everything I do until I am called to that eternal banquet where war is no more, and You are all in all.

Amen.

# Chapter VIII

**Night Prayers of Protection**
*"You will not fear the terror of night…"* – Psalm 91:5

# VIII.I Prayer to Close Spiritual Portals

Lord Jesus Christ,
As darkness falls and silence wraps the world, I come to You once more—not in fear, but in faith. I bring to You this day in its entirety: every word spoken, every image seen, every thought entertained. I ask You now to close every spiritual portal that may have been opened, knowingly or unknowingly, through sin, carelessness, or exposure to what is unholy.

If I have invited darkness through what I watched, read, heard, or welcomed in conversation, I now renounce it in Your holy name. If I have participated in gossip, spoken in anger, consumed violent or impure content, or allowed bitterness to dwell in my heart, I ask Your forgiveness and cleansing. Let no doorway remain open to the enemy. Let no invitation linger in the spiritual realm. I cancel every claim and shut every gate that does not belong to You.

Cover my body, my mind, and my spirit with Your Precious Blood, Lord Jesus.
Let it rest like a seal upon me as I sleep. Let Your Blood flow over the walls and thresholds of this room, saturating the space with Your presence and peace. Let every corner be guarded,

every shadow be filled with light, every place be consecrated to You alone.

Holy Angels of God, I invite you now to surround my bed. Stand watch at every door and window. Defend me from the enemy who prowls in the dark. Shield my sleep from torment, disturbance, or fear. Let no unclean spirit approach. Let no nightmare take hold. Guide my dreams toward what is pure, and let the night hours restore what the day has wearied.

I give this night to You, Lord.
Let it be holy. Let it be sealed. Let it be safe. May I rise in the morning renewed, protected, and strengthened for the work ahead. And if You should call me home before the dawn, may I wake in the arms of mercy.

In the name of Jesus Christ, my Savior and Deliverer,
I close every door to darkness, and I rest under the mantle of Your love.

Amen.

## VIII.II The Litany of Light

Jesus Christ, Light of the world,
Shine now into the shadows of this night. I invoke You, not with trembling, but with trust. You are the Light that darkness cannot comprehend, the flame that never dies, the dawn that no night can overcome.

Light of Truth, illumine my mind.
Light of Mercy, calm my soul.
Light of Glory, dwell in my heart.

Where fear has crept in, drive it out. Where anxiety clings, let it dissolve in Your radiance. Where confusion clouds my thoughts, bring clarity. Let Your Light pierce every lie, silence every whisper of despair, and dismantle every wall of isolation.

Jesus, Light of the nations,
Shine in every room of my heart and every corner of my memory. Break the chains that fear has forged. Scatter the oppression that steals rest. Let not a single power of darkness speak into this night, for You are here, and You are Lord.

Light of Bethlehem, who came in the stillness,
Light of Calvary, who shone through the Cross,
Light of the Resurrection, who shattered the tomb—
Shine now upon my life, and be the lamp that burns through every hour until morning comes.

I surrender the night to You,
with its silence, its dreams, its mysteries, and its peace.

Be the Light that surrounds me, the Light that defends me, the Light that leads me even while I sleep.

Amen.

## VIII.III Prayer of Peace for the Household

Holy Spirit, Breath of God,
I invite You now into this home. Not only as a guest, but as Lord. Hover over these walls, pass through each doorway, rest upon every bed, and sanctify each space where life unfolds. Let Your peace be like oil poured in abundance—gentle, healing, and enduring.

I speak now the peace of Christ over this household.
Over the **entryway**, that no evil may cross the threshold.
Over the **living room**, that all conversation be seasoned with grace and unity.
Over the **kitchen**, that every meal be blessed and every gathering be kind.
Over the **bathrooms**, that even the simplest acts be done with dignity and gratitude.
Over the **bedrooms**, that they become places of true rest, not anxiety, not fear, not unrest. Let all **nightmares be cast out**, let **insomnia be broken**, and let a holy stillness settle over every pillow and every soul.

I renounce the spirit of unrest.
I break its hold in the name of Jesus Christ.
Let all disturbance be scattered. Let all spiritual noise be silenced. Let no foothold remain for anger, fear, sorrow, or discord. Let this home be claimed entirely for the Kingdom of God.

Come, Holy Spirit, and reign here.
Speak into the walls. Flow through the halls. Breathe upon each

soul. Anoint this place until every heart within it knows peace, and every visitor senses Your presence.

Let angels stand guard at every corner.
Let saints intercede at every hour.
And let the Lamb of God be enthroned in every heart and every home.

In the name of Jesus, Prince of Peace,
this house is Yours, tonight and always.

Amen.

# Chapter IX

**Intercessory Prayers for Others in Battle**
*"Bear one another's burdens..."* – Galatians 6:2

# IX.I Prayer for a Loved One in Crisis

Lord Jesus Christ,
You who see every heart and know every soul by name, I come to You on behalf of one I love, who now walks through darkness, confusion, or pain. You are never far, even when we feel lost. You are never silent, even when the world grows loud. I ask You now to draw near with power, with tenderness, and with divine precision.

Intervene, O Lord—not by force, but by mercy.
Break through whatever wall has been built. Speak through the noise. Shine light into the places they may no longer see. Whether the battle is one of the mind, the body, the heart, or the spirit, let Your healing and truth surround them. Let no lie remain. Let no chain stay locked. Let no fear reign where Your love longs to dwell.

I offer my suffering, however small or hidden, as a spiritual ransom for their soul.
Take every tear I have shed, every sleepless night, every silent ache, and unite it to Your Passion. Let this offering rise as a plea for grace. May it open a door in Heaven that no darkness can shut. Do not let the enemy claim even a moment more of

their life. Redeem what has been lost. Restore what has been broken. Return what has been taken.

I bind this loved one to Your Sacred Heart, Jesus.
Not by force, but in intercession. I wrap them in prayer and plead the Precious Blood to cover them. Let no evil come near them. Let no voice of despair take root. Let Your mercy speak louder than every regret. Let Your light reach even to the furthest corner of their soul.

I do not ask for easy answers, but for holy transformation.
If healing must come through suffering, let it be redemptive. If clarity must come through trial, let it lead to You. If silence must remain for a season, let it prepare the way for Your voice.

Jesus, I entrust them entirely to You.
You love them more than I ever could. You see what I cannot. You wait at the door even now. Go to them. Speak to them. Stay with them.

And until they are made whole,
let me carry their name in prayer without ceasing.

Amen.

# IX.II Prayer for Those Under Spiritual Attack

Lord God of Hosts,
I lift up to You those now under spiritual assault—whether seen or unseen, spoken or hidden. You know their hearts, You know their wounds, and You see the battle that surrounds them. In the name of Jesus Christ, I speak Your Word over their life: *"No weapon formed against you shall prosper"* (Isaiah 54:17).
*"Greater is He who is in you than he who is in the world"* (1 John 4:4). *"The Lord is my light and my salvation—whom shall I fear?"* (Psalm 27:1).

I stand in the gap, O Lord, and I rebuke the enemy in the name of Jesus.
I renounce every unclean spirit that seeks to oppress, deceive, confuse, tempt, or torment them. Let the shadows be scattered. Let every curse be broken. Let every lie fall to the ground. In the power of Christ's victory on the Cross, I claim their deliverance. Let the Blood of Jesus speak louder than accusation. Let His mercy be their defense.

I call now on the angels of Heaven to surround them—Michael, great prince of the heavenly host, defend them in battle. Gabriel, messenger of the Most High, declare truth to their heart. Raphael, healer of God, anoint their wounds and guard their rest. Let legions of angels, sent by the Father's will, drive back every force that seeks their ruin.

Holy saints of God, pray for them.
Saint Joseph, protector of the Church, guard their home and mind.
Saint Teresa of Ávila, teacher of inner warfare, guide them

through the shadows.
Saint Padre Pio, marked by suffering, intercede for strength and peace.
Saint Joan of Arc, holy warrior, inspire courage in the heart of battle.

Lord, let Your Spirit rest upon them now.
Let them not grow weary. Let them not fall to despair. Send them companions in the fight, voices of encouragement, and moments of sacred clarity. Bring victory, not by might, but by grace. And when the battle is long, be their shelter and their shield.

I entrust them to You, O Christ, for You are faithful.
You will never leave them, never forsake them, never abandon those who cry out in need.

Amen.

## IX.III Prayer for the Church Under Siege

Eternal Father,
Your Church, born from the side of Christ and sealed in His Blood, walks now through fire. Across the earth, Your faithful are mocked, hunted, silenced, and slain. In homes, in workplaces, in parishes, and in the public square, the enemy sows confusion and fear. But still, the Bride of Christ stands. Still she prays. Still she loves.

I lift to You now the persecuted Church.
For those imprisoned for the name of Jesus, send angels to guard them. For those facing death, grant courage unto the end. For hidden believers who gather in secret, let their praise thunder louder in Heaven than cathedrals ever could. For families torn apart by the cost of faith, bring healing and reward their fidelity.

Purify Your Church, Lord—not with destruction, but with holy fire.
Cleanse what is corrupt. Expose what is hidden. Bring to repentance what has grown cold or compromised. May every trial refine her. May every blow drive her deeper into Your truth. Let her unity be forged not by human strategy, but by shared suffering and sanctified hope.

I pray now for our priests—protect them from scandal, temptation, and discouragement. May they be men of prayer, fathers to the flock, and fearless proclaimers of the Gospel. For bishops, grant wisdom and fortitude. Let them lead not for the world's approval but for Heaven's reward. And for the laity, strengthen our resolve to remain faithful, to speak truth, to live holiness in the midst of a fading culture.

Let the Church on earth reflect the Church in Heaven—
a multitude clothed in white, washed in the Blood of the Lamb, victorious through the Cross. Let no force on earth prevail against her. Let no division undo her mission. Let no night snuff out the light You placed within her.

Jesus, Shepherd and King,
preserve Your Bride until the day You return in glory.
Until then, make us holy. Make us ready. Make us fearless.

Amen.

# Chapter X

**Victory and Praise – Living in Triumph**
*"But thanks be to God, who gives us the victory through our Lord Jesus Christ." – 1 Corinthians 15:57*

# X.I Prayer of Praise for Breakthrough

Almighty and Ever-Faithful God,
Before the battle ends, before the storm is still, before the final stone is rolled away, I lift my voice in praise. I worship You not for what I see, but for what I know to be true. Your promises are not delayed. Your power is not diminished. Your love has never failed me.

I praise You, Lord, for the breakthrough that is already written in Heaven.
Though I do not yet see the victory with my eyes, I declare it with my heart. You are the God who parts seas, who topples walls, who speaks and mountains move. You are not bound by time, not shaken by enemies, not silent when Your children cry out. In the very place where fear once stood, I now raise a song.

I praise You with the words of the Psalms, for they are my weapons in the waiting.
*"The Lord is my light and my salvation; whom shall I fear?"*
*"I waited patiently for the Lord; He turned to me and heard my cry."*
*"You prepare a table before me in the presence of my enemies."*
These are not verses of comfort only—they are war cries of the

faithful. I sing them not in retreat, but in defiance of despair. I speak them not to escape, but to conquer. I believe that what You have begun, You will bring to completion.

I rejoice in the unseen because You are already there.
You have gone before me. You stand beside me. You fight within me. And You are my song. Even if the enemy surrounds me, I will not be moved. Even if the delay is long, I will not lose heart. Even if I stumble, Your mercy will lift me again.

So I praise You now, Lord—
in weakness and in waiting, in hope and in faith, in the tension between promise and fulfillment. Because You are good. Because You are faithful. Because You are God.

Let this praise shake the walls of fear. Let it open the gates of grace. Let it be incense before Your throne. Let it be the sound of triumph before the final trumpet sounds.

To You be all glory, all honor, all dominion, all praise.
In the name of Jesus Christ, who has already won every victory I will ever need.

Amen.

# X.II Declaration of Identity in Christ

Lord Jesus Christ,
I come before You now not in uncertainty, but in truth. I cast down every lie spoken over me, every word of defeat, every voice that told me I am unworthy, unlovable, powerless, or alone. In Your name, I renounce the false names I have believed—rejected, forgotten, weak, broken, impure. I am not who the enemy says I am. I am who You say I am.

I am a child of God.
I have been bought with a price, redeemed by the Blood of the Lamb. I am not a prisoner of the past, not a slave to sin, not a victim of fear. I am a new creation in Christ. The old has passed away; the new has come.

I am a warrior in the army of the Most High.
I have been given armor, not to hide, but to stand. I wear the belt of truth, the breastplate of righteousness, the shield of faith, the helmet of salvation, and the sword of the Spirit. I walk in the authority of one who has been commissioned by Heaven.

I am an heir with Christ, seated with Him in the heavenly places.
I am not abandoned. I am adopted. I am not overlooked. I am chosen. The Spirit Himself bears witness with my spirit that I am a child of God. I have access to the throne of grace, boldness in the presence of my Father, and inheritance that will not fade.

I declare what the Word of God says:
I am more than a conqueror through Him who loves me.
I can do all things through Christ who strengthens me.

I am the salt of the earth and the light of the world.
I am God's workmanship, created in Christ Jesus for good works.

Lord, seal this identity in my heart.
Let no voice shake it. Let no wound undo it. Let no lie distort it.
Let me walk forward from this moment knowing who I am—
not by merit, but by mercy. And let this truth be a banner over every day that lies ahead: I belong to You.

Amen.

Spiritual Warfare

# X.III Litany of Victory

Christ our King,
You have conquered sin and death. You have crushed the serpent's head beneath Your heel. You have shattered the gates of hell and risen triumphant from the tomb. To You belongs all victory, all glory, all dominion. Today I proclaim not only what You have done—but what You are still doing, in me and in Your Church.

Through Your Cross, I am free.
Through Your Resurrection, I have hope.
Through Your Ascension, I am raised with You.

Saint Michael the Archangel, victor in battle—pray for us.
Saint Peter, rock of the Church, who triumphed through tears—pray for us.
Saint Paul, fearless in chains and faithful unto death—pray for us.
Saint Mary Magdalene, who rose from ashes into witness—pray for us.
Saint Perpetua and Saint Felicity, who sang on the way to the sword—pray for us.
Saint Joan of Arc, holy warrior of truth—pray for us.
All martyrs, confessors, virgins, apostles, and mystics—pray for us.
You who overcame by grace—stand with us as we press on.

Lord Jesus, the battle is Yours, and the victory is complete.
The tomb is empty. The veil is torn. The serpent is crushed. The throne is occupied.

Your name is exalted above every other name. And in Your name, I now rejoice.

I celebrate the triumph of the Kingdom of God—
not only in the heavens, but in hearts being set free today. In lives reclaimed. In nations yet to bow. In quiet sanctity and bold proclamation. In the hidden faithful and the great cloud of witnesses.

Victory is not a feeling. It is a fact, written in blood and sealed in glory.

I praise You, Lord of hosts.
I magnify You, Lamb of God.
I rejoice in You, risen and reigning King.

Yours is the Kingdom.
Yours is the power.
Yours is the victory—now and forever.

Amen.

Spiritual Warfare

# Conclusion

**Stand Firm**

The battle is not over—but neither is the grace. You have been given prayers not as poetry, but as weapons. You have spoken truth in a world of lies, called on Heaven in a time of noise, and surrendered to God when the world urges self-preservation. This prayer book is not the end of the fight—it is your beginning.

Stand firm.

Pray daily, not as a task but as your breath. Let morning rise with consecration. Let night fall with trust. In moments of joy and moments of trial, turn again to the words that remind you who you are: a child of God, armed with mercy, guarded by angels, and sealed with the power of the Cross.

Do not neglect the sacraments. Confession is your cleansing. The Eucharist is your strength. The Word of God is your sword. Stay close to them. Let them renew you. Let them sharpen your vision, your courage, your love. Return again and again to the altar, not only to receive—but to be transformed.

Do not fight alone.
The Church is your family. The saints are your witnesses. The angels surround you. When the darkness thickens, find the voice of the faithful. When temptation presses, speak the name of Jesus aloud. When you feel weak, receive again what He freely offers: grace, peace, and strength beyond your own.

And above all, remember this:
You are not alone. Heaven fights with you.
The battle belongs to the Lord. The victory is already written.
You stand not on sand, but on a rock.
You pray not into a void, but into the heart of the living God.

So take courage. Keep praying. Keep fighting.
Let the flame never go out.
Let the cry of your soul be heard again and again—until, at last,
faith becomes sight, and the warfare gives way to glory.

Amen.

www.ingramcontent.com/pod-product-compliance
Lightning Source LLC
Chambersburg PA
CBHW051703090426
42736CB00013B/2523